Given for You

Other books in the Lutheran Voices series

See www.lutheranvoices.com

Given for You
Reflections on the Meaning of the Lord's Supper

Louis W. Accola

Augsburg Fortress

Minneapolis

GIVEN FOR YOU
Reflections on the Meaning of the Lord's Supper

Copyright © 2007 Augsburg Fortress. All rights reserved. Except for brief quotations in critical articles or reviews, no part of this book may be reproduced in any manner without prior written permission from the publisher. For more information visit: www.augsburgfortress.org/copyrights or write to: Permissions, Augsburg Fortress, Box 1209, Minneapolis, MN 55440-1209.

Scripture quotations, unless otherwise marked, are from the New Revised Standard Version Bible, copyright ©1989 by the Division of Christian education of the National Council of the Churches of Christ in the U.S.A. Used by permission. All rights reserved.

Pages 23 and 53 contain portions of The Small Catechism by Martin Luther (Minneapolis: Augsburg Fortress, 1979). Used by permission. The Confession on page 52 and the Post-Communion Canticle on page 57 are ©1978 Lutheran Book of Worship, admin. Augsburg Fortress.

Cover Photo: Loaf of bread on table in wheat field © Goodshoot/Corbis

Library of Congress Cataloging-in-Publication Data
Given for you : reflections on the meaning of the Lord's Supper / edited by Louis W. Accola.
    p. cm.
ISBN 978-0-8066-5365-5 (alk. paper)
1. Lord's Supper—Meditations. I. Accola, Louis W., 1937-
BV826.5.G58 2007
264'.041036—dc22
                    2007023265

Large-quantity purchases or custom editions of this book are available at a discount from the publisher. For more information, contact the sales department at Augsburg Fortress, Publishers, 1-800-328-4648, or write to: Sales Director, Augsburg Fortress, Box 1209, Minneapolis, MN 55440-1209.

The paper used in this publication meets the minimum requirements of American National Standard for Information Sciences—Permanence of Paper for Printed Library Materials, ANSI Z329.48-1984.

Manufactured in the U.S.A.

11 10 09 08 07 1 2 3 4 5 6 7 8 9 10

This book is dedicated to all who gather at the Lord's Supper and to my family and friends who sit with me at meal tables where we are nourished for the day and the journey we share.

Contents

Preface

I had two main purposes for writing this book. First, I wrote it as a teaching resource for members and inquirers in Christian congregations, to refresh and to enhance our understanding of the meaning of Jesus' special meal. As a teaching and preaching resource, this book can be an insightful and helpful read for anyone wanting to reflect on the holistic meaning and gospel-centered use of the Lord's Supper. My hope is that through personal reflection and group discussion, this book may foster growth and transformation in Communion practices and encourage and support open, inclusive, and full intercommunion practices in and between Christian congregations. The book is also written in a format that lends itself for this enrichment and transformational ministry through a sermon series, an adult class series, book discussion group, or as a focus and study book for a retreat on the meaning and use of the Lord's Supper.

Secondly, I wrote this book to lift up and to restore the importance of the sacrament of the Lord's Supper as one of two major weekly actions in our Christian liturgy—Word and Sacrament—regardless of the variety of liturgical settings being used in worship services. I believe that the Lord's Supper is not to be just an add-on when there is enough time in the allotted worship time. This sacrament—commonly called Holy Communion because its simple elements are so sacred and special as the real presence of Jesus' body and blood through the bread and wine—is not to be seldom used. Some limiting and restrictive perspectives and teachings on the use of this sacrament need to be put aside, such as if received too frequently the Supper might be misused, be taken too lightly or unworthily, or become too familiar and casual. Our rich worship heritage is Word (grace read and proclaimed) and Supper (grace visually seen, touched, and tasted) together, making up the two major foci of our liturgy.

The writing of this book has a long history. It began years ago as a series of adult classes on eleven facets of meaning for the Lord's Supper that I wrote for a congregation I was serving in Milwaukee, Wisconsin. These eleven facets were gleaned from rereading my class notes from Dr. Kent Knutson, a favorite mentor and my professor for a course on church doctrine at Luther Seminary in St. Paul, while I was a student there. This adult class series was shaped and reshaped a number of times and then used as a summer sermon series for a congregation I served in Perrysburg, Ohio. In that congregation we were addressing two concerns related to the use and sharing of the Lord's Supper, namely, the age for first communion of children and the new practice of open communion for all baptized, communing Christians worshiping with us. In 1996, I turned what I had previously written into a Lenten sermon series on "The Supper of the Lamb" for the parish family I was serving in Woodinville, Washington. The next year, the content of that series was published by Vantage Press in New York, under the title, *The Supper of the Lamb: Reflections on the Meaning of the Lord's Supper*. Now, the material from that book has been reshaped yet again into the volume you are reading today.

This book is intended for both personal reflection and group use. To that end, questions for discussion are included at the conclusion of each chapter. Pastors may want to consider using this book in a sermon series during Lent or during a discussion on the meaning and use of the Lord's Supper, or perhaps rise to the timely challenge of a discussion on the Lord's Supper with a neighborhood group of congregations reflecting an ecumenical mix of participants.

For further study, a glossary and a list of resources, including books, videos, and websites, are included at the end of this book. Although the selected list is not exhaustive, it is meant to point the way for those who want to go through a historical review of the theological issues and practices of Holy Communion and who wish to learn more about the sacrament and how it is celebrated in the church. As we further implement new agreements for Communion practices among Protestant churches and continue to move toward intercommunion practices between Protestant and Catholic parishes, this book may be a helpful resource in the continuing renewal and transformational journey.

It is my hope that this book will broaden and deepen your understanding and experience of the Lord's Supper. As we move quickly through the first decade of the twenty-first century—a turbulent, broken, and warring decade—it is time to let this Supper be shared openly, freely, and joyfully. In doing so, we affirm both the nourishment and the transformational power that comes to us in this meal. Sharing this meal together can express, nourish, and expand the unity that is *a given reality* and *a gift* to us by God's creating and doing. It is our privilege and deep joy to participate in it!

Acknowledgments

I would like to take this opportunity to thank those important persons in my life and ministry who have encouraged me and have been the inspiration for writing my first book, *The Supper of the Lamb*, and this book, as well. I am indebted to my mentor at Luther Seminary, the late Dr. Kent Knutson, for the eleven facets of meaning for the Lord's Supper that provided the vision and conceptual framework for my writing and guided my interest and concerns for further study, research, and reflection on the meaning and the use of the Lord's Supper in our personal lives and congregations. Dr. Kent Knutson died an untimely death from a rare disease contracted while on a tour of global mission work in New Guinea. Kent nurtured my theological foundations and perspectives still basically affirmed in this book—though honed and matured in clarity and practice. This publication is shared in grateful remembrance of this outstanding theologian, teacher, and leader in our Lutheran Church.

I also acknowledge with gratitude the many authors of books and articles that I have read on the issues addressed in this book. They all have in some way inspired and nurtured my understanding of the meaning and use of the Lord's Supper. While the pages of this book are not peppered with names and direct quotes from other writers, I remain grateful to these mentors. I acknowledge their significant enrichment in my preaching and teaching on Communion and their broadening of my understanding and pastoral use of the Lord's Supper.

I want to thank Kathy Corneloup, my church secretary at Wooden Cross Lutheran Church, Woodinville, Washington, for her supportive enthusiasm and extra work hours spent typing several drafts of the original sermon series into a book manuscript. Without her creative assistance, my first book on the Lord's Supper—the book on which this one took form—may not have been completed.

I am equally grateful at this time of publishing *Given for You* for my Augsburg Fortress editor and her vision for this book. Her enthusiasm and creative spirit, insights, guidance, and encouragement through the writing and publishing process of this book were most appreciated.

Most of all, I want to thank my wife Kathy, my best friend and companion on this journey through life, for her constant enthusiasm, encouragement, and support through the time consuming task of writing. I also thank Kathy for her computer knowledge and skills that have assisted me so much in my writing.

This book is shared with deepest gratitude for my family who sit with me at the meal tables in our homing places and favorite restaurants, who are special and loved just for who they are for me—my wife Kathy, our young adult twins Katie and Kent and Kent's companion Emily, and our three adult sons, Terence, Steven, and Hans with his wife Bella and my first granddaughter Charlotte Louisa, who join us for special milestones and celebrations.

Finally, this book is shared with gratitude for all brothers and sisters, mentors, peers, and friends, who have and who continue to gather somewhere at the best meal in town—the Lord's Supper, and by so doing keep the Supper's proclamation, gifts, and promises experienced today and passed on for the life of the world and future generations.

Introduction

Some of my fondest early memories are of my grandmother over a stove fixin' food for our daily feast.

I grew up eating well. Cheese grits, homemade biscuits smothered in butter, home-cured ham, red-eyed gravy—and that was just breakfast. Smothered chicken, butter beans, fried corn, and cornbread was a typical weekday dinner. Sunday supper (when the preacher from the church down the road would often stop by) was a celebration. Food was the guest of honor, covering so much of the table there was hardly room for plates.

—Oprah Winfrey (*In the Kitchen with Rosie: Oprah's Favorite Recipes*, [New York: Knopf], 1994, p. xi)

The Best Meal among Our Meals

Meals are a part of the daily routine of people in every culture, community, and household around the globe. Food is our common ground. Gathering around the table to eat meals together and to take part in mealtime rituals is a universal experience. What we eat directly affects our health and total well-being. We all have heard the expressions, "Here, eat this! It's good for you!" or "One of life's greatest pleasures is eating and drinking!" or "You are what you eat!" At one time or another, all are true.

For many daily eating revolves around three meals, commonly called breakfast, lunch, and supper or dinner. An especially celebrative meal might be called a party or a fiesta. A very elaborate meal of many courses, with formal dress attire, fine linens, china and silverware, might be called a banquet or a feast. Our school children often take a small meal, called a snack, with them for extra nourishment through another school day.

Most communities and cultures care about those without daily bread, so there are food drives and food banks. There are soup kitchens for the homeless and many programs to provide a daily meal for shut-ins. These meals are for the nourishment of our physical well-being. The fellowship around meal tables in homes, restaurants, and community centers nourishes our relationships and emotional bonds and provides opportunities to express a caring presence and acts of supportive or celebrative love.

My wife and I have rich memories of arriving at my mother Joyce's house with our children after a five-hour drive from Perrysburg, Ohio, where we lived from 1984-1992. Not only were we and our children welcomed with open arms and with hugs and kisses, there also was a banquet ready for us. Every meal seemed like Thanksgiving in my mom's house in Slater, Iowa. My mother would lovingly prepare one or two kinds of meat, mashed potatoes and gravy, two kinds of vegetables, "glorified rice," along with fresh dinner rolls, pickles, and other relishes—and, of course, the necessary Lutheran fruited Jell-O salad to make this meal a complete and acceptable feast. The freshly baked cherry or apple pie, with vanilla ice cream, was just an extra.

God has given a new feast to the human family. The menu is not as elaborate as the one my mother would put together. God's feast is just a piece of bread, usually unleavened, and a small cup of wine or grape juice. It is God's meal for God's global people. Through this meal God shares with us some nourishment for our life and relationships, for our well-being and faith and renewal along life's daily journey, and for our hope of a destiny beyond this life.

It is the best meal in town because it is for everyone, with blessings for today and promises for tomorrow, that is, for beyond the end-time of each of our journeys in this world as we know and experience them from our human points of view. This meal, with Jesus as the only host, announces, gives, empowers, and promises all people what God has done and continues to do for the life of the world through the paschal lamb Jesus. It is God's action and blessings through Jesus that makes all people the invited ones, the worthy ones, and the accepted ones.

We are all guests at this meal. Every participant, each time at this table, is a guest. There is no other role or criteria for being welcomed at the Lord's Table. The Lord's Supper is God's doing and menu for us. When the Supper is celebrated and shared, the invitation should be to all God's daughters and sons and participated in for the life of the world. We do not participate in this meal just for our own personal benefits, nourishment, and salvation. Each time we also proclaim God's saving work accomplished through Jesus.

It is my conviction that as central as forgiveness is to the meaning and purpose of the Lord's Supper, the meal instituted by Jesus for the church and for the life of the world is more. The Supper is like a beautiful diamond with many facets that together give the gem its wholeness in value and beauty. This book seeks to explore the facets of meaning in the Lord's Supper. The Lord's Supper, then, reminds us each time we participate that our lives are shaped by the future God has already prepared for us. That is the deeper mystery for us to ponder as we explore together these facets of the Supper's meaning for us today. You will be reminded for whom the meal is meant and how it is to be shared. Attention is given to its benefits for all who receive it for themselves and for the sake of the whole human family that God has loved into a new, lasting relationship and promise in the life, death, and resurrection of Jesus.

It is my hope that, as you read this book, the simple earthy meal of bread and wine will become a more meaningful, joyful, inclusive, and often-celebrated meal for you and your faith community. Ponder with me in these five chapters God's presence, God's grace, God's forgiveness, God's healing, and God's promise for tomorrow—the many faceted gifts that come to us through Jesus' simple meal.

Forgiveness enables us to live with our yesterdays, our painful memories of things done or left undone.

1

The Lord's Supper Is a Meal of Forgiveness

So he set off and went to his father. But while he was still far off, his father saw him and was filled with compassion; he ran and put his arms around him and kissed him. Then the son said to him, "Father, I have sinned against heaven and before you; I am no longer worthy to be called your son." But the father said to his slaves, "Quickly, bring out a robe—the best one—and put it on him; put a ring on his finger and sandals on his feet. And get the fatted calf and kill it, and let us eat and celebrate; for this son of mine was dead and is alive again; he was lost and is found!" And they began to celebrate. (Luke 15:20-24)

We begin this consideration of the Lord's Supper with one of Jesus' most familiar parables, that of a wayward son, an envious brother, and a forgiving father who loves both. While this may not be an obvious place to begin, there are good reasons for doing so. For instance, the activity in the parable, like that of the Lord's Supper, centers on a meal. In the parable, the father hosts a lavish banquet—replete with fatted calf—to celebrate the return of his prodigal son. While the bit of bread and sip of wine that we receive in the Lord's Supper hardly qualifies as a banquet in any stretch of the imagination, it is, nonetheless, a celebratory meal made possible by a Father's love for his wayward children.

In Jesus' time, to invite another person to eat with you was to say, "I accept you." This explains why Jesus caused such controversy when he dined with tax collectors and sinners. They were the outcasts of society, the unacceptable ones. In choosing to eat with them, Jesus proclaimed, "I accept you. God accepts you." Jesus believed, as did the Jewish people, that every opportunity to eat together was a sacred occasion.

Jesus' generous acceptance of all is evidenced powerfully in the faces of those who gathered at table with him on the night before his death. His invitation to "Come, eat. Come, drink," was extended to all—Judas the betrayer, Peter the denier, Thomas the doubter, as well as the other ordinary, sinful men whom he called disciples. None were excluded for their lack of understanding or their failings of character. At that last supper, Jesus ushered in the day when all people are invited to dine at table with the host who is also the meal, the bread and wine of the supper. The invitation, the blessings, and the promises attached to this meal are for everybody. Our Lord says so.

Forgiveness Poured Out

There is another reason for us to begin this book with the parable recorded in Luke 15. While most often referred to as the "Parable of the Prodigal Son," Jesus' story is more importantly about a forgiving father. It is, after all, a forgiving father "filled with compassion" who runs to meet his wayward son. It is a forgiving father who embraces his son without waiting first to hear what he has to say for himself. It is that same forgiving father who calls for the celebration to begin because the prodigal has returned.

Do you see where this is going?

Have you ever known another person whom you couldn't stand? Have you ever made a decision not because it was right or fair but because you hoped it would get you what you wanted? Have you ever been mad at someone and shared your anger with everyone in town except the person with whom you were angry? Have you ever been jealous of the accomplishments of a friend or work associate?

We are all too familiar with the role of the prodigal, because we recognize ourselves in his selfish and self-centered actions. We can also identify with the envious older brother who could not see beyond his sibling's foolish irresponsibility to appreciate his father's overwhelming love for both sons. We stand in need of God's gracious forgiveness even while withholding forgiveness from others. This is what makes this meal of forgiveness even more remarkable.

In the Lord's Supper we hear again the promise of God's love for us poured out in the blood of Jesus for the forgiveness of our sins—though we do not deserve it. No wonder that the Lord's Supper has become the central act of Christian worship. In the words, "Come, eat. Come, drink," we hear the gospel—the good news—proclaimed again and again. Because of Jesus, we are all welcome at the Lord's Table. Because of Jesus, all is forgiven.

What do we mean when we say that all this is "because of Jesus"? Luther's meaning to the second article of the Apostles' Creed explains:

> At great cost [Jesus] has saved and redeemed me, a lost and condemned person. He has freed me from sin, death, and the power of the devil—not with silver or gold, but with his holy and precious blood and his innocent suffering and death. (*The Small Catechism in Contemporary English*, Augsburg Publishing House and Fortress Press, 1979)

Our acquittal was won by Jesus on the cross. To any who would accuse us, Jesus says, "These people belong to me. They are mine! If you have something to take up with any one of these people, tell me about it!" To us, Jesus says, "You have been forgiven. Go and do likewise."

Because real sins have real consequences in this life, forgiveness is as necessary to life as is air or water. No relationship, whether between parent and child, siblings, spouses, friends, co-workers, or neighbors, can survive without forgiveness.

Forgiveness enables us to live with our yesterdays, our painful memories of things done or left undone. Forgiveness gags the mouth of our past, which, like an obnoxious acquaintance, shows up to tell stories about us that were best forgotten long ago. In Jesus' forgiveness we are empowered to reconcile with a dying parent, to settle up with an estranged son or a daughter, to face a former spouse or a conflicted work associate. In Jesus' forgiveness we are free to let go of the resentments, the recriminations, the rehearsals of revenge that we harbor toward others.

More than that, when Jesus forgives, he forgets. Jesus doesn't even seek to identify the offender. That is what the Apostle Paul meant in his pastoral letter to the Christian community in Rome when he affirmed, "There is therefore now no condemnation for those who are in Christ Jesus" (Romans 8:1). Jesus remembers our offenses no more.

When Jesus forgives we are granted a different future—a future no longer shaped by our past but shaped, instead, by the one responsible for forgiving. Jesus' forgiveness gives each of us a new identity through the means of the bread and wine in this simple meal. Here Jesus announces a new basis for our relationship with God and with one another. Here Jesus declares that our future no longer comes simply out of our past as consequence or reward. Now our future opens out of Jesus' unfolding hands and gift.

When Jesus forgives he promises that as he has taken control of what has happened he also controls what will happen to us in the future. Jesus will shape our future on the basis of his gracious, free, and unconditional care for us. When Jesus forgives we go forward confidently, in peace, toward our future. We anticipate that no matter what has happened in our past and no matter what our today will bring, Jesus will turn all things to our good in the eternal season of our "bread for tomorrow."

Forgiveness as Gift

Forgiveness is not deserved, nor can it be earned. It is gift. "But wait," we say, "what about the wayward son in the parable? Didn't he have to make the first move?" It's true. The prodigal came to his senses. Broke, starving, and humiliated, the prodigal determined to return home, admit his sin to his father, and ask to be treated as a hired hand. "Doesn't his repentance count for something?" we ask.

Jesus obviously thought repentance was important. According to Matthew's Gospel, Jesus' first words at the beginning of his public ministry were, "Repent, for the kingdom of heaven has come near" (Matthew 4:17). These can be harsh words, uncomfortable words, even offensive words to hear if we take them seriously and understand them to be directed to us personally. It is difficult for us to name our wrongs to others, not least of all to God. We often are reluctant and slow to acknowledge responsibility for our sinful thoughts and actions. On the other hand, we are quick to point out the failings of others.

A story is told about a father whose work responsibilities made it impossible for him to join his wife and young daughter on a trip to Grandma's house. "I'm sorry that I can't go with you," he explained to his disappointed little girl, "but Daddy has to stay home and check his invoices." Later that day, the little one announced to her grandmother, "Daddy couldn't come because he's having trouble with his conscience."

Luther recognized that outward acts such as fasting and confession of sins serve a good purpose as we prepare to receive the sacrament. Listening to our "inner voices" and taking stock of what we have done to wrong others is a useful exercise, as long as we put this in perspective. Our acts of repentance and our attempts to ease our guilty conscience are not prerequisites for receiving the forgiveness that is given with the bread and wine of the Lord's Supper. No,

Luther says in his explanation of the Lord's Supper in the *Small Catechism*, "that person is well prepared and worthy [to receive the sacrament] who believes these words, 'given and shed for you for the remission of sins.'"

The gift comes by faith. We need to guard against the idea that dining at the Lord's Table is a reward for confessing sins and begging forgiveness, for if understood in this way, the sacrament becomes an exercise in fulfilling the law. Instead, we need to understand that even our confession is in the hands of God, as the writer of Psalm 51 so beautifully expressed:

> Create in me a clean heart, O God,
> and put a new and right spirit within me.
> Do not cast me away from your presence,
> and do not take your holy spirit from me.
> Restore to me the joy of your salvation,
> and sustain in me a willing spirit. (Psalm 51:10-11)

When Jesus began his ministry by calling the people to "Repent, for the kingdom of heaven has come near," he did not intend for the people to heap up sacrifices to cover wrongdoings—an impossible task in itself. Rather, Jesus' call to repentance was a call to be open to receive the kingdom with its rich blessings, promises, and inheritance for all. Mark's Gospel records Jesus as saying, "The time is fulfilled, and the kingdom of God has come near; repent, and believe in the *good news* [gospel]" (Mark 1:15, italics added). That is, repent, for the presence of God is at hand to do and to accomplish something mighty special for you and for all people.

Repentance is itself a gift of the Spirit of the Living God who helps us to see just how much we need God's gracious forgiveness and who helps us celebrate the presence of God in our lives through the simple gift of a piece of bread and a sip of wine. The Spirit helps us to see in this simple meal that the coming of the kingdom is the coming of God, the Word made flesh, full of grace and truth. The One present to do the will and the work of God the Creator for our salvation is the One present in our experience of the Lord's Supper. "Repent! Be open! Turn with a receptive eye and heart," Jesus calls to us. "I am here with you and for you. I am your Bread of Life, now and forever!"

When repentance is seen as something we do rather than something God works in us, "true" repentance seeks validation in outward signs of sorrow and contrition for failing to be the people God intended us to be. Unfortunately, morbid introspection on our moral failure to live up to God's law leads to fear that God will reject us—and rightfully so—at both the Lord's Table and the banquet feast to come. From the perspective of the law, we participate in the Lord's Supper to make amends for guilty consciences. We partake of the bread and wine as persons condemned by our sins rather than as sinners forgiven and saved.

The Lord's Supper is certainly for the repentant—for all who recognize the need for God's presence and forgiveness—for all who understand that while we live in grace as God's kingdom people already, we also live in sin as human beings. Our need for forgiveness is great, indeed, and so we do well to come frequently to the Lord's Table where the reality that the kingdom of God is upon us is announced, celebrated, and experienced in each and every meal.

How and When Do We Come?

I remember a social event in a previous parish when the conversation turned to the appropriate manner for approaching the Lord's Table. It was noted that some came very reverently, with eyes downcast and hands folded. Others held their arms against their bodies, or tucked their hands in their pockets. Some, especially children, came forward relaxed and smiling, with arms swinging. A few made the sign of the cross on their forehead or their chest upon receiving the bread and wine. Finally, one member turned to me and asked, "Pastor, what are we supposed to do with our hands?"

I responded, "Do whatever feels right to you, and do not worry about it." What matters, after all, isn't how we come but that we come.

Participation in the Lord's Supper needs to be a regular part of the Christian's life. Do we eat only when it is convenient to do so? No, we make time in our busy lives to eat because we understand that our bodies need nourishment regularly if we are to live lives of faithful witness to the one who invites us to "Come, eat." Do we come to the table only when we feel especially needful of God's forgiveness or the assurance of God's presence? No, for while it is certainly right to come at such times, if we reserve the sacrament for only such occasions, we deprive ourselves of its benefits for our daily lives. And so we come often to the table, in faith and in joy, trusting in God's mercy and clinging to Jesus' promise that all that is provided is, indeed, "given for you" and for me, and for all who partake of his body and blood—and for the sake of those who are not even there.

Living Forgiveness and Sharing It with Others

The Lord's Supper is a meal of forgiveness, but the benefits of the forgiveness granted in and through the supper extend beyond those who partake of the meal. In the experience of being forgiven, we are empowered to forgive others.

Living God's Word given to us through Jesus' body and blood in the Lord's Supper should be of utmost importance for us in our daily relationships. The bread for which we pray in Jesus' model prayer, "Give us this day our daily bread," is that which we receive in his simple supper. It is bread for today and for tomorrow. It is the Bread of Life that forgives and empowers us to reach out to others in the world today through our daily acts of love, justice, and right doing.

We pray in Jesus' prayer: "Forgive us our sins as we forgive those who sin against us." Knowing that we are the forgiven ones at the Supper, we are to be forgiving and affirm in daily living Jesus' way of forgiveness. This hearing and doing can impact us—and others through us—with that same love and renewing, healing power that Jesus brought into various situations in his day. Jesus apparently knew that those who were part of the faith community bearing his real presence and name would make mistakes, engage in disputes, and harbor wrongdoings. No one likes disappointments, misunderstandings, and hurts. We dislike conflict even more in our personal lives and within our church families. Jesus' response to such conflict is recorded in Matthew 18, where he provided a pattern and a procedure for dealing with these inevitable sins and wrongdoings.

We are reminded here that Jesus regarded forgiveness as central and the costly way of our discipleship for our life together in a Christian community. Confused a bit by Jesus' proposed pattern for handling disagreements, concerns, and conflict, Peter asked Jesus in this teaching: "Lord, if another member of the church sins against me, how often should I forgive? As many as seven times?" (Matthew 18:21). Jesus' response was: "Not seven times, but, I tell you, seventy-seven times" (Matthew 18:22).

Here we have from Jesus a procedure for dealing with these inevitable wrongdoings and disputes (Matthew 18:15-20). First, the one offended is to take the initiative. The one offended is to bring up the issue or concern directly and privately with the offender. We notice here a basic principle for maintaining relationships—whether in friendships, in families, in workplaces, in neighborhoods, or in God's household called the church. The one who has been wronged is not told, "Be silent. Go ahead and nurse your hurt or your anger privately." No, even though the one offended is probably quite convinced that the offender consciously started the problem, the one offended is the one responsible to take the initiative for the conversation.

What do we see here in Jesus' pattern? We see that Jesus holds each of us responsible for our feelings and reactions—as well as our actions. Jesus is aware here that such a disruptive and destructive pattern needs to be replaced with his pattern of resolution and forgiveness. Jesus is saying here that it is the responsibility of the one offended to be honest and up front about his or her feelings and concerns. The person offended, upset, or hurt should not wait for someone else to figure it out and take care of it. In Jesus' way, every effort is to be made within this most direct way and level of communication.

There is, however, a sense of realism in Jesus' awareness and teaching. Therefore, if there is no resolution, Jesus says: "Take your issue, your hurt, or your concern to the second level by gathering one or two others to listen." Jesus is here suggesting that a neutral third party or someone in the community who is known to be wise in such matters is sought out to listen and to help the parties discern together for a good resolution.

We have here another basic principle in maintaining and growing open, healthy relationships in the many arenas of our lives: Involve a neutral third person or group when necessary. The point here is, if the direct approach doesn't get a response or doesn't resolve the conflict, appropriate steps should be taken, rather than allowing the problem to become a matter of household or public grumbling, gossip, or combat, resulting in more festering until it becomes disruptive. Here we might also remember the Apostle Paul's cautioning words: "For the wages of sin [broken relationships/wrongdoings] is death [disruption or destruction], but the free gift of God is eternal life in Christ Jesus our Lord" (Romans 6:23).

Finally, if this does not achieve resolution, Jesus' pattern for life together in Christian community is to take the matter to the church leaders. If this final effort falls short "and if the offender refuses to listen even to the church, let such a one be to you as a Gentile and a tax collector" (Matthew 18:17). That is: an outsider.

This admonition as the final step in Jesus' pattern of discernment and forgiveness does not sound much like Jesus, and the focus in this chapter, does it? It is a most difficult admonition to affirm and to practice in our personal lives and in the life of our community together. Perhaps Jesus is saying that, for the time being, such a person is choosing to be like "an outsider" to God's demonstrated way in Jesus. Therefore, by choice, he or she has put himself or herself in this situation.

Indeed, this closing admonition does not sound like the Jesus we know from so many other scenes in the Gospels. Jesus always left the door open a crack to let the possibility and the power of forgiveness operate. We recall Jesus' words to Peter, "Not seven times, but, I tell you, seventy-seven times," and his other teachings: "Whenever you stand praying, forgive, if you have anything against anyone; so that your Father in heaven may also forgive you your trespasses" (Mark 11:25); "Do not judge, and you will not be judged; do not condemn, and you will not be condemned. Forgive, and you will be forgiven" (Luke 6:37).

So what are we to make of all of this? The most important part for us today—far more important than the pattern and the procedure itself that is laid out by Jesus—is the spiritual context in which this teaching is to be pursued and practiced. If we read the earlier verses of chapter 18 in Matthew's Gospel, and the verse following this teaching, it becomes clear that the only appropriate resolution and disciplinary pattern in any of our relationships is childlike humility and unending forgiveness.

The spiritual climate for any of these conversations and our pattern of living in daily relationships is to be one of humility, compassion, and unending forgiveness. Indeed, that is always the bottom line for Jesus in all situations—for both "the insiders" and "the outsiders." Forgiveness was and always is God's action expressed toward the whole human family in Jesus. Not just once. Not just seven times. Not even seventy-seven times. But, now and eternally so!

Forgiveness is God's big embrace of the whole human family. We are all the offenders, for we all have fallen short of the glory of God. Through Jesus, God took both the initiative to tell us so and the action to cancel out the final consequences for all our offenses. Jesus taught that forgiveness is without limit and does not exclude anyone. God's forgiveness keeps on forgiving—right on into eternity! Like in the old, familiar camp song we love to sing, "He's got the whole world in his hands," we are all in God's grace-filled hands. We are all recipients of God's forgiveness. That's the good news we are given at the supper of forgiveness.

To be forgiven, to experience that forgiveness at the Lord's Supper, to live in forgiveness, and to live forgivingly toward others as a way of life—whether they recognize their need or even seek forgiveness—is to participate in the mystery of God's love. Perhaps that is why the saying rings so true: "To err is human; to forgive divine."

Jesus knew that we all are sinners and that we all are sinned against—even within God's church family. Forgiveness in Jesus' way tugs us beyond the place where we only want to view ourselves as righteous, as right over against God and others. Forgiveness in Jesus' way encourages us to give more than we planned to give in our situations and relationships. We take our example from Christ who gave us his all—his very life—on the cross for all people, where he spoke those absolution words for our sake and the sake of the world: "Father, father—forgive every last one of them." And each time we receive the Lord's Supper, God's meal of forgiveness, we experience again Jesus' word to us personally and for the sake of the whole human family: "Father, father—forgive every last one of them."

Questions for Discussion

1. What was the meaning of a meal in Jesus' day? What did it mean to invite someone to dine with you? How does that compare with our present-day understanding of sharing meals together?

2. How can receiving the Lord's Supper help when you are being difficult or when you are upset with another person? Who does it help—you or the other person or both?

3. What is involved in being ready and receptive at the Lord's Table? How do you personally prepare to receive this gift?

4. Who is welcomed at the Lord's Supper? With whom should we share this meal?

5. What does it mean to you that, "We are all sinners, yet saved"?

6. How is what we experience and receive at the Lord's Supper to be lived out in our daily lives and relationships?

In this remembrance, we see that God acts in bread and wine, in flesh and blood, in the person Jesus, to make known and real to us God's redeeming love and forgiveness.

2

The Lord's Supper
Is a Sign of Remembrance

For I received from the Lord what I also handed on to you, that the Lord Jesus on the night when he was betrayed took a loaf of bread, and when he had given thanks, he broke it and said, "This is my body that is for you. Do this in remembrance of me." In the same way he took the cup also, after supper, saying, "This is the new covenant in my blood. Do this, as often as you drink it, in remembrance of me." For as often as you eat this bread and drink the cup, you proclaim the Lord's death until he comes. (1 Corinthians 11:23-26)

Bread and wine—these humble elements shared by Jesus' disciples in an upper room in Jerusalem, and for generations after wherever Jesus' followers gather—hearken back to an earlier occasion marked with another meal. The Exodus, chronicled in a biblical book by the same name, was the formative event in the history of the Israelite people. It lives on in the collective memory of generations who faithfully keep the annual Passover festival as God commanded them to do. "This day shall be a day of remembrance for you. You shall celebrate it as a festival to the Lord; throughout your generations you shall observe it as a perpetual ordinance" (Exodus 12:14).

Why is "this day" so important?

It was on "this day" that the Hebrew people smeared lambs' blood on their doorposts as a sign of their faithfulness to God. It was on "this day" that the homes of the faithful were passed over and the inhabitants were spared from death. It was on "this day" that God intervened on behalf of God's beloved children to free them from bondage in a foreign land.

For centuries following the Exodus, the annual slaying of the Passover lambs, eating the Seder meal, and retelling the events of "this day," composed a powerful remembering for the Jewish people. The Passover signified for each person the gift of God's deliverance in the past, in the present, and in the eternal tomorrow yet to come. This is the context in which we begin our reflections on the Lord's Supper as a sign of remembrance.

A New Deliverance

In Jesus' day, faithful Jews from distant cities, near-by villages, and the surrounding countryside, made the annual pilgrimage to Jerusalem to participate in the most important festival of the year, the Passover. They came, as their ancestors had come before them, to offer sacrifice at the Temple and to share the Seder meal. They came, not realizing that this Passover would be different from all the rest because of a man named Jesus. On a steady course to his crucifixion, Jesus would enter the city to change the heart of its people, to change the heart of a nation, to change the heart of the world.

He came riding a donkey—borrowed for the occasion—into a city occupied by Roman troops, to a people oppressed. Surely some who witnessed Jesus' entrance remembered the words of the prophet Zechariah centuries earlier, "Lo, your king comes to you; triumphant and victorious is he, humble and riding on a donkey, on a colt, the foal of a donkey" (Zechariah 9:9). Certainly some wondered if the prophecy was soon to be fulfilled. Could this be the long awaited Davidic king who would once again sit on the royal throne in Jerusalem?

In the twenty-first chapter of Matthew, we read that the crowd along the main road leading into Jerusalem on that day turned the annual festival pilgrimage into a messianic demonstration. Perhaps incited by Jesus' disciples or inspired by a living hope that the long-awaited Messiah had finally come, the people began to sing loud "Hosannas." Some spread their cloaks on the road before him. Others cut branches from the trees, shouting, "Hosanna to the Son of David!" Remembering an earlier deliverance in the distant recesses of their history, they called out for another: *Save us now, Son of David! Save us now!*

Later that evening as they gathered for a meal in the upper room, Jesus gave his disciples bread to eat, saying, "This is my body given for you. Do this in remembrance of me." Then he bade them drink the wine "in remembrance of me." In doing so, he instituted a new "remembering" of a deliverance soon to come, a deliverance from slavery to sin and death. As in the Exodus, this deliverance would be accomplished through the blood of a lamb. But not just any lamb. The blood of this lamb belonged to Jesus, the Lamb of God, who died once and for all for the deliverance of all people of every time and place.

Eating "in Remembrance"

Take, eat. Do this in remembrance of me. Take, drink in remembrance of me. These familiar words are proclaimed every time we come to the Lord's Supper. But what does this eating in remembrance mean?

When we reflect on the Lord's Supper, we tend to return only to the scene played out in the Upper Room on the evening of Jesus' betrayal. But in the closing chapter of Luke's Gospel (Luke 24:13-35), there is another story about the power of memory and remembrance that provides insights into what it means to eat and drink in remembrance of Jesus.

The gospel writer tells us that on the Sunday following Jesus' death, Cleopas and another of Jesus' disciples traveled the road from

Jerusalem to Emmaus, a journey of about seven miles. Frightened, confused, no doubt discouraged, even disillusioned by the sudden and unexpected end to their hope that Jesus was the long-awaited Messiah, they puzzled together about all that had happened.

Then the risen Jesus joined them on the road, though they did not recognize him. Since the man appeared to be unaware of all that had so recently transpired in Jerusalem, they assumed that he was a stranger in the area. As they walked together, the disciples related to him the events of the previous week. In keeping with Jewish hospitality toward strangers, as they drew near to their destination at the close of the day, they invited him to eat and stay the night with them.

Imagine what Jesus' disciples were thinking and feeling as they gathered around the table. As the day ended, all they had left were their memories of Jesus and a rumor that on that very morning some women from among Jesus' followers had discovered his tomb empty. This report had disturbed them profoundly, for they had not yet seen Jesus.

Now, gathered around the table, they observed as the stranger took a piece of bread. He blessed it. He broke it. He shared it with them in a familiar way. Luke reports that in this moment, "Their eyes were opened, and they recognized him" (Luke 24:31). In the breaking of the bread, the disciples became aware that the man at table with them was Jesus, their Risen Lord.

After the meal Jesus did not stay with them, but "vanished from their sight," leaving the disciples to reflect together on all that they had experienced. "Were not our hearts burning within us while he was talking to us on the road, while he was opening the scriptures to us?" they marveled (Luke 24:32). So today we experience our "hearts burning within us" each time bread is blessed and broken and these words of promise are proclaimed: "This is my body given *for you.*"

Jesus accomplished in the breaking of the bread to move the disciples from fear to faith in his risen presence and promises.

Whenever God's people participate in this special meal, we affirm the real presence of our risen Lord revealed just as surely as it was to those at table with him in Jerusalem and Emmaus—revealed to us in, with, and under bread broken and wine poured, according to his command to *do this in remembrance of me.*

The Meaning of the Sacrament

What does it mean to say that the people of God today celebrate the Lord's Supper *in remembrance* of Jesus? To answer this question, we will seek to clarify what it does not mean.

First, we must realize that what occurs in the Lord's Supper is not, in any sense, a redoing of Jesus' sacrifice. Nor is it a re-presenting of Jesus to God. Such understandings make the sacrament into a human work performed to merit God's favor and acceptance, something already accomplished once and for all in Jesus' death and resurrection. To suppose that to *do this in remembrance of me* means that the benefits of the sacrament are dependent somehow upon our offering of the bread and wine—Jesus' body and blood—disregards the fact that God has the primary role in the meal, as God does in our salvation. To do this is to put the biblical order of things in reverse. It is to believe that we act in order to experience redemption.

Jesus' command, *do this in remembrance of me,* invites us to see that God has acted and continues to act in bread and wine, in flesh and blood, in the person Jesus, to make known and real to us God's redeeming love and forgiveness. If the Lord's Supper is to be experienced as grace—God's grace—then we must realize that to *do this in remembrance of me* refers not to our offering of the elements—the bread and wine—but to our receiving of those elements and the gifts God provides in this holy meal. The primary action in the Lord's Supper is from God to us, not from us to God.

Secondly, we must also understand that to *do this in remembrance of me* is not simply our recalling of an event that happened more than two thousand years ago. This understanding relegates the Lord's Supper to little more than an opportunity to think upon the last meal Jesus shared with his disciples, wherein we are simply reminded of Christ's death for us. In this understanding, almost nothing is thought to be happening in the sacrament. That is, nothing is happening apart from our remembering, and the benefit of the Supper consists of whatever blessings our memory provides.

As in the first misconception, this understanding also leads us to believe—wrongly—that we, not God, are the primary actors in the sacrament. If our activity—our recalling of the meal Jesus instituted on the night before his death—is the means to receiving the benefits of the Supper, what does this mean for believers who have been robbed of their memories by dementia, disease, or accident? Does the loss of memory negate the benefits of the sacrament? Of course not! Again, we must remember who the host is at this Supper. We must remember to whose Supper we have been invited. It is to the living God, not to us, that this redeeming, this renewing action primarily belongs.

Why Do We Participate in this Holy Meal?

While our primary focus has been on the question, "What does it mean to eat and drink in remembrance of Jesus," perhaps it is important to ask, "Why do this at all?" Certainly by now it is abundantly clear that God's saving activity in our lives and in the world is neither merited by nor dependent upon our actions. So why do we eat and drink in remembrance of Jesus?

We do so because he told us to. In Lutheran understanding, a sacrament is defined in part as an act instituted by Jesus' command. This definition applies to Holy Communion and it also applies to Baptism, as we discover in the Great Commission where Jesus says, "Go therefore and make disciples of all nations, baptizing them in the name of the Father and of the Son and of the Holy Spirit, and teaching them to obey everything that I have commanded you" (Matthew 28:19-20).

But we don't observe the sacraments simply because Jesus tells us to. By definition, the sacraments include earthly elements given along with God's Word of promise. In the Lord's Supper, the visible elements are bread and wine, and as we eat and drink and hear the words spoken, "given and shed for you," we trust that Christ is really present with us. In the faithful practice of receiving the Lord's Supper, God's saving activity and gifts are forwarded through the sacred meal from the distant past to today, and God's abiding presence is made real with us and for us. We experience and realize, through all of our senses, the visible means of receiving Jesus' presence into our bodies through the bread and wine.

Finally, every time we gather at the altar or around the font, we hear proclaimed God's promise of forgiveness, salvation, and eternal life. This blessing and promise are precisely what was given to the disciples in Jerusalem, in Emmaus, and everywhere else that the Supper has been shared and will be shared until Christ comes again. When we gather at the Lord's Table and listen to what has been proclaimed through the ages, "This is my body given for you; this is my blood shed for you," we remember times in our lives and in the lives of others when these words of promise provided hope in despair, comfort in sorrow, forgiveness in failure, and assurance in fear.

Indeed, to celebrate the Lord's Supper *in remembrance of Jesus* means emphatically that God here and now ushers into the present what Jesus has done in the past—provided the final and complete sacrifice for the salvation of the world and for each of us in its future.

Truth be told, Jesus doesn't need the Supper. We do.

In our eating and drinking *in remembrance of him,* we are assured time and time again that he will, indeed, *remember us.* For this is our fear, isn't it? That Jesus will forget us. That his promise of presence is for others, but not for us. That we have sinned so often or so heinously that he can no longer find it in his heart to forgive us. Like the thief on the cross, we cry out, "Jesus, remember me!" Even the thief, whether in his time or in eternity came to know that "nothing can separate us from the love of God in Christ Jesus" (Romans 8:39).

What Memories Do We Bring to the Table?

Each time we come to the Lord's Table, we bring with us personal memories of this meal.

Memories of...

eagerly receiving the bread and wine for the very first time;

celebrating the sacrament in the intimate setting of a spiritual retreat;

sharing the Supper for the last time at the bedside of a dying loved one;

being present with a son or daughter at their First Communion;

joyfully breaking bread with friends around a crackling campfire;

eating and drinking in Jesus' name with believers in a foreign land;

gathering around the Lord's Table with family members home for the holidays.

Breaking the bread and passing the cup stirs our memory and opens our eyes to see the living Jesus, so present, so near, so real. Indeed, the Lord's Supper is a means of remembrance.

Questions for Discussion

1. What are the similarities and the differences in the Seder meal and the Lord's Supper as a remembrance meal?

2. What does it mean to you now to say that the Lord's Supper is a sacrificial meal?

3. What does your reflection on this chapter's facets of understanding about the Lord's Supper imply about the frequency for
Holy Communion? Do you think it should be celebrated once a
month, whenever there is time in the Liturgy, as an annual meal
like the Seder meal, or as frequently as possible?

4. How is the Lord's Supper a source of personal renewal? Of community renewal?

5. How is the Lord's Supper a personal experience, but more than a
personal experience?

We don't come to the Lord's Table with something to offer—our worth, our perfection, our understanding, our possessions, our praises, even our lives. We come bearing nothing only to receive everything. This is gospel alone! It is for this reason that the Lord's Supper is identified as a means of grace.

3

The Lord's Supper Is a Means of Grace

While they were eating, Jesus took a loaf of bread, and after blessing it he broke it, gave it to the disciples, and said "Take, eat; this
is my body." Then he took a cup, and after giving thanks he gave it
to them, saying, "Drink from it, all of you; for this is my blood of
the new covenant, which is poured out for many for the forgiveness of sins. I tell you, I will never again drink of this fruit of the
vine until that day when I drink it new with you in my Father's
kingdom." (Matthew 26:26-29)

We are a people living by grace. God's grace. We often find the
gracious acts of God in the ordinariness of God's creation—in water
and bread and wine. Matthew's Gospel recounts how in the simple
sharing of bread and wine, Jesus provided a means by which God
would establish a new covenant with humanity. Jesus' broken body
and shed blood would usher in a new day of grace and a foretaste
of the life all who believe will share in God's eternal kingdom. That
God's promise would be contained in such common earthly elements as bread and wine is remarkable, but more remarkable still
was the powerful promise based on God's loving action in Jesus. The
disciples could not have grasped the full meaning or impact of Jesus'
words. The events foreshadowed in the meal were yet to unfold.

Matthew's Gospel concludes the description of the last supper
shared by Jesus and his disciples with these words: "When they had

sung the hymn, they went out to the Mount of Olives" (Matthew 26:30). It was there in a tranquil garden called Gethsemane that the events leading up to Jesus' crucifixion began to accelerate.

"Remain here, and stay awake with me," Jesus asked his disciples that evening before going a little ways away to pray (Matthew 26:38). Later, after praying fervently that he might be relieved of what was to come, or if not relieved, then empowered to do his Father's will, Jesus returned to find his followers asleep. Rousing them he implored them a second time, "Stay awake and pray that you may not come into the time of trial; the spirit indeed is willing, but the flesh is weak" (Matthew 26:41). Jesus knew of what he spoke. Twice more he returned to discover that his disciples could not keep their heavy eyes open even as the time of his betrayal, arrest, trial, and death grew nigh.

Like the weary disciples in the garden, we, too, have failed to be faithful. We have been distracted by our desires and the desires of the world around us and have strayed from God's way and from God's love. But God has not strayed from us. So as we approach the Lord's Supper it is important that we remember to which mountain it is that we come.

We do not come to Mount Sinai with its memories of the law and its judgments that impugn our acts—"If you, O Lord, should mark iniquities, Lord, who could stand?" (Psalm 130:3). We come instead to Calvary, the "holy mountain" where our Savior died. We come as people saved not by our own doing, but by God's amazing grace. We come freed from the judgment that we deserve under the law by what God has done for us and for all people through Jesus' sacrificial death.

The good news of the gospel is that in Jesus God comes to us. "This is my body given for you," Jesus says, "This is my blood shed for you." The direction is clear. In Jesus, God's grace is poured out upon us. This is gospel alone!

The gospel is not our attempts to understand, to interpret, to debate who Jesus is and what Jesus is able or unable to do for us and for our salvation. We don't come to the Lord's Table with something to offer—our worth, our perfection, our understanding, our possessions, our praises, even our lives. We come bearing nothing only to receive everything. This is gospel alone! It is for this reason that the Lord's Supper is identified as a *means of grace*.

God's Word and the Sacraments of Baptism and Holy Communion are called the "means of grace" because they are the vehicles God uses to reveal the promises that are for us. Through these means, the Holy Spirit graciously works within us to create faith. In them, God calls, nurtures, and strengthens us and the whole community of believers. They are the means of *grace* because they are not based on anything we do or have done, but rather because they bear God's gift of new life for us.

Gospel, not Law—God's New Covenant Relationship with Us

The Bible is the story of God's covenant relationship with God's people, a relationship defined in the Old Testament by obedience to God's law. At supper on the night before his death, Jesus announced a new covenant relationship based not on our obedience but on God's forgiveness "poured out for many" in Jesus' blood.

Those who gathered to share the Passover meal with Jesus that evening were not perfect men who measured up to the standard of God's law. If that were the case, what would be the need of the gospel? They weren't included because they somehow had earned the privilege of breaking bread with Jesus. Nor were they excluded from the meal because of things they had done or failed to do. They were there as his guests. They were given a place at the table because of their relationship with him and because of their need to be forgiven. The same is true for us. We can do nothing to merit either the invitation to the Lord's Supper or the benefits received there. The Supper is God's gracious gift to us through which we realize God's visitation in the now of our existence. As we eat the bread, drink the wine, and hear the promise, "This is my body, given for you. This is my blood shed for you," we experience in a very real and visible way Jesus' presence with us.

Let there be no doubt that we are saved by God's grace in Christ Jesus and not by our obedience to God's law. But law in and of itself is not bad. God gave the law as blessing, to bind his people to one another and to himself. When asked which of the commandments was the greatest, Jesus replied, "You shall love the Lord your God with all your heart, and with all your soul, and with all your mind" (Matthew 22:37). But he didn't stop there. He added a second commandment that connects us to one another: "You shall love your neighbor as yourself" (Matthew 10:38). In those two commandments, Jesus summed up the whole of the law. And so it was that he lived his life.

It is when we compare ourselves to Jesus that we realize our desperate need for God's forgiveness. It is in the presence of the one whose image and way of life is both judgment and blessing upon us, that we recognize our sin. It is then that we fall on our knees and beg for God's mercy.

> Most merciful God, we confess that we are in bondage to sin and cannot free ourselves. We have sinned against you in thought, word, and deed, by what we have done and by what we have left undone. We have not loved you with our whole heart; we have not loved our neighbors as ourselves. For the sake of your Son, Jesus Christ, have mercy on us. Forgive us, renew us, and lead us, so that we may delight in your will and walk in your ways, to the glory of your holy name. Amen (*Lutheran Book of Worship*, p. 56)

The Bible is very clear that no one is without sin: "If we say that we have no sin, we deceive ourselves, and the truth is not in us. If we confess our sins, he who is faithful and just will forgive us our sins and cleanse us from all unrighteousness" (1 John 1:8-9). It is customary in many churches to make public confession of one's sins prior to receiving Holy Communion. In the presence of God and one another we admit that we have all fallen short of our calling to love God and neighbor. We admit our need for God's mercy.

For centuries after the Reformation, private confession was also encouraged prior to receiving the sacrament. According to *Luther's Small Catechism*, while we should confess all sins, known and unknown, to God, "in private confession, as before the pastor, we should confess only those sins which trouble us in heart and mind." Luther goes on to say that we can examine our daily lives according to the Ten Commandments, asking ourselves "whether we have been disobedient or unfaithful, bad-tempered or dishonest, or whether we have hurt anyone by word or deed."

There are at least two important points that we must recall in any honest and meaningful act of private confession whether directly to God, to a pastor, to a counselor, or to a trusted friend. First, the quality of our confession does not depend on the length of the list of sins we compile. If this were the case, what would happen if one forgot a sin or two? Or what would be the penalty for intentionally omitting a sin? Such arithmetic only distracts from the gravity of a whole life turned away from divine purpose. What is needed in confession is the honest recognition of one's condition in life, of one's total dependence on God's mercy. As the psalmist reminds us, "A broken and contrite heart, O God, you will not despise" (Psalm 51:17).

The second point we need to remember is that our need for forgiveness is not evidenced in comparing ourselves with one another. Too often the result of such comparisons is that we come to the conclusion that next to "so and so," we're pretty good after all! We become like the Pharisee who stood in the temple and prayed, "God, I thank you, that I am not like other people: thieves, rogues, adulterers, or even like this tax collector." Meanwhile "that tax collector," aware of his sinfulness, broken in spirit, and bowed down before the Lord, prayed, "God, be merciful to me, a sinner!" (Matthew 18:11-13).

No, our guilt is not evidenced in comparing ourselves with one another. Rather, it is made visible in relation to Jesus, the Christ, with whom we have all been identified in our baptisms. The Lord's Supper offers us a personal and communal opportunity to open ourselves to receive into our very lives the God who seeks to make all things new—even us. So it is that our relationship with Jesus begun in our baptisms is renewed in the Lord's Supper. It is strengthened. It is deepened. It is fed. We come to the Lord's Table hungry for purpose, meaning, and reconciliation. In this meal we hear again and again the host's words of grace, "You are absolved. You are forgiven," as we take into ourselves the one who, through his death and resurrection, reconciles us to God and to one another.

We can prepare for coming to this meal. We can pray. Some traditions fast, withhold eating until after participation in the Lord's Supper. We can read the Bible. We can spend time in meditation, reflecting on the special gifts received in this meal. We can confess our wrongs, big ones and minor ones. We can go to private confession and hear the words of forgiveness, even before going to this meal. These are all helpful ways to prepare for open, meaningful, and receptive participation. But none make us worthy of the Lord's Supper.

Assured of God's Love, We Can Respond with Joy

In the Lord's Supper we receive a visible sign of God's grace that is ours in Christ Jesus. Sometimes, however, we need a little touch, a little reminder, that we are indeed welcome at the Supper, and that something good and helpful actually happens in our eating and drinking. We are not unlike the child who stands at the side of a pool and fearfully declares, "No! I don't want to go into the water! I'll drown…and you will be sorry!" With a little coaxing, the parent finally convinces the child to come into the shallow end of the pool and, in no time at all, the child is gleefully blowing bubbles and dogpaddling to her heart's content.

Then the day comes when the parent encourages the child to jump into deeper water with the gentle assurance, "Remember, I'll be right beside you all the way." And so the child jumps, but the water is deep, and the child's swimming skills are rudimentary, and soon she begins to sink. It is then that the parent puts a hand under the child's stomach and gives the child a little lift, and all at once the child is swimming.

The Lord's Supper is for all who are in over our heads, all who are fearful of failure, drowning in despair, sinking in sin. "Remember," Jesus gently assures us, "I'm here with you. This bread is my body. This wine is my blood. I am with you always."

After supper on the night of his betrayal and desertion, denial and alienation, as all the anxiety, greed, hate, and fear of the world settled squarely on his shoulders, Jesus assured his followers of his love for them saying, "As the Father has loved me, so I have loved you; abide in my love" (John 15:9). He went on to speak of joy, "I have said these things to you so that my joy may be in you, and that your joy may be complete" (John 15:11) and to assure them that the joy of which he spoke was an eternal joy, "So you have pain now; but I will see you again, and your hearts will rejoice, and no one will take your joy from you" (John 16:22).

Participation in the Lord's Supper with our risen Lord empowers us to walk joyfully in newness of life even as we continue life's journey as forgiven people in a sin-filled world. In this simple meal we remember Jesus' death on our behalf and we celebrate the presence of our living Lord with us on this day and everyday.

We read a number of times in the book of Acts about how the early Christian community gathered together frequently in joy and gladness with thanksgiving to break bread together. Because of their faith in a risen Christ present with them in the very experience of the Lord's Supper, they were a joyful fellowship. We, too, are to be filled with joy in our table fellowship at what surely is the best meal in town.

Given all this, I wonder why our joy isn't more evident as we leave the Lord's Table? I've noticed that many who come to the table with solemn expressions, leave the same way. Are they concerned that somehow their confession was incomplete or that it lacked the appropriate degree of contriteness? Is it that they have not heard or do not believe that they have been absolved of their sins? Or does the occasion seem to them too solemn to smile?

Perhaps the word *holy* attached to our time of communion with one another and God in Jesus' presence is a hindrance to our joy. Surely this is the case if *holy* is misunderstood to refer to a perfect, whole, harmonious community of people. But to speak of *Holy Communion* is to acknowledge not who or what we are but whose we are—a fellowship of God's forgiven sons and daughters united and called out in Jesus for life and mission together in the world today.

Does this ultimately have to do with whether we see ourselves as Good Friday Christians or Easter Christians? Certainly we believe that Jesus' death on the cross was necessary for our redemption. But Good Friday is incomplete without Easter. Without the resurrection, Jesus' death on the cross—one of thousands of such deaths meted out as Roman justice—would have mattered not for our lives today or our lives to come. But Jesus' innocent suffering and death did matter. He took upon himself our sin and gave his life for ours. But our faith, our joy, is in knowing that it is the risen Christ, the one who claims victory over death, who comes to us in the bread and wine shared in this holy meal.

We are not like the young Luther who knew only a judgmental, angry God. If this were the God we encounter in the Lord's Supper, we would be right to be solemn. Even fearful! But as Luther ultimately discovered, the righteousness of God is God's right to declare us forgiven ones in Jesus. Our encounter is with the One who says, "Listen! I am standing at the door, knocking; if you hear my voice and open the door, I will come in to you and eat with you, and you with me" (Revelation 3:20).

The verdict is already in—*acquitted!* This is the good news, the gospel. It is the news rejected as foolish by many people and confused as cheap grace by others. But to quote the Apostle Paul, "I am not ashamed of the gospel; it is the power of God for salvation to every one who has faith....For in it the righteousness of God is revealed through faith for faith; as it is written, 'The one who is righteous will live by faith.'" (Romans 1:16-17).

If the Lord's Supper is truly a *means of grace*—and it is—then the benefits of this meal come to us through no efforts of our own. We, who are not worthy even to gather up the crumbs from under the table, are welcomed into the presence of God and fed with a holy food. Forgiven, nourished, and refreshed, we depart to serve others on behalf of the One who has served us, in a world hungering for grace, thirsting for hope, seeking life in its fullest.

> *Thank the Lord and sing his praise; tell ev'ryone what he has done.*
> *Let ev'ryone who seeks the Lord rejoice and proudly bear his name.*
> *He recalls his promises and leads his people forth in joy with shouts of thanksgiving.*
> *Alleluia, alleluia.*

(The post-communion canticle, *LBW* p. 115)

Questions for Discussion

1. What must we do to be worthy of receiving the Lord's Supper?

2. How does our understanding of this sacrament being a gospel meal shape, and possibly change, our communion practices?

3. What *laws* were used to exclude people from the Lord's Supper in your childhood? How and why were they appropriate or inappropriate?

4. Compare Good Friday Christians and Easter Christians. What importance is this clarity of understanding for our mood and practices of celebrating the Lord's Supper?

5. Why is joy an appropriate emotion for receiving the Lord's Supper?

6. Why do crosses in Lutheran Churches rarely have the figure of a dying Christ on them? What significance might this have for the meaning and the mood of celebrating the Lord's Supper in these settings?

It is our privilege and our responsibility, having been nourished with Jesus' body and blood, to depart from the Lord's Table to act on behalf of Jesus, the Living Bread, to feed a world hungry not only for a meal but for meaning, hungry not only for today but for tomorrow.

4

The Lord's Supper Is a Source of Life for the World

"I am the living bread that came down from heaven. Whoever eats of this bread will live forever; and the bread that I will give for the life of the world is my flesh." (John 6:51)

Because we work long hours to earn money to pay for the things we need, it's easy to forget that all that we have is God's gift to us. When I come as the Lord's guest to the Table, I am reminded that the food offered in this meal—a bit of bread and a sip of wine—is but a tiny portion of the food that God provides. I am reminded, too, of all the other things God provides to sustain us in our lives here and now. I leave the Table refreshed and nourished, trusting in the Living Bread to provide the daily bread that I need.

But Jesus promises that *whoever eats of this bread will live forever.* No matter how hard we try to extend our days and preserve eternal youthfulness, the fact is that we can't create our own eternal future. This, too, is God's gift to us. And so, I am reminded each time I partake of the Lord's Supper that God provides not only for our temporal existence but for everlasting life as well—our bread for today and our bread for tomorrow.

During the Israelites journey from slavery in Egypt to freedom in the Promised Land, God provided sweet water to quench their thirst and manna to quiet growling stomachs. For forty years, they were nourished and strengthened by this "bread from heaven" that appeared miraculously in the early morning and melted away as the sun rose higher in the sky. Generations later, the Israelite people continued to look upon bread as a sign of God's abiding presence. In the daily breaking of bread and in the annual Passover meal, they were reminded of God's faithfulness in the past and they remembered God's promise to be with them in their present day lives as well.

This awareness helps us understand why bread is a central symbol in Jesus' teaching, especially in the Gospel of John. Here in Jesus' saying, "I am the living bread," we are reminded that the Word that "became flesh" in the Christmas incarnation was nailed to a cross on Good Friday to die an innocent death on behalf of a sinful world and then rose from the dead on Easter. Jesus' claim, "I am the living bread," assures us that because he lives, we may live also—but such assurance isn't offered exclusively. It is "for the life of the world" that the Living Bread came down from heaven (John 6:51).

Jesus' teaching in the Gospel of John points to the supper he shared with his disciples on the night before his death and beyond to the meal believers through the ages have shared and will continue to share in Jesus' name. In this reflection on the Lord's Supper, we will explore how the benefits of this meal extend not only to those who participate in the Supper but also to the whole world.

The Presence of God in the Lord's Supper

It's easy to see why the men in the synagogue in Capernaum had no idea what Jesus was talking about when he spoke of himself as living bread. There was no way prior to Jesus' death and resurrection that they could understand his claim. So, unable to grasp the big picture, they began to argue among themselves, asking, "How can this man give us his flesh to eat?" (John 6:52).

This question does beg for an answer. After all, Jesus had made a fantastic claim. From our post-Easter perspective we understand that Jesus' teaching points to his sacrificial death on the cross and to the meal we share in remembrance of him. But this is a difficult teaching even for us, and it raises other questions. "How is Jesus present in the bread and wine of the Lord's Supper?" we wonder. "How is Jesus able to be present in the Lord's Supper when it is celebrated simultaneously in faith communities all over the world?"

Ultimately, I think we are asking in these questions and others like them whether God is real and, if so, is God really present in our lives and in the world. Especially in these times of escalating violence in our homes, communities, and the world, we yearn for reassurance that the answer is a resounding, "Yes!"

I remember a conversation in which a professing Christian man told me how he had narrowly escaped a serious automobile accident. He was driving down a busy city street, somewhat unfamiliar to him, when he came to a congested intersection. Failing to see the traffic signal change at the corner, he ran the red light and was just missed being hit by a car whizzing by from the cross street. He concluded his account by saying, "Praise the Lord! God was really with me there! God helped me through my own carelessness."

I have no doubt that God was present in that moment, as God is present in every moment of our lives. But how was God present? Did God step in at the last moment to rescue a driver from his own carelessness? What if there had been an accident? Would that mean that God was absent in that moment? Would it signify God's inability—or unwillingness—to act in that particular instance?

But let's return to the question posed in John 6:52. The Jews in the synagogue that day who asked, "How can this man give us his flesh to eat?" understood Jesus to be speaking literally. But this literal understanding misses the point, for it is not only Jesus' flesh and blood but the whole of the life of Christ that is received in the eating and drinking of the Lord's Supper. Such a God is not content to be present only in times of urgency, as when careless drivers run red lights. Nor is God content to come and go at our bidding, for we all know there are times when we really would prefer that God weren't quite so present. Rather, in the intimacy of this relationship, God dwells within us shaping our thinking, molding our motives, guiding our words and actions, claiming us as his own, and saving us from ourselves to live for others.

It's true that God is present in some way in every moment, but God has committed to us in Jesus to be present in a special, intimate way in this meal. I don't know how this is accomplished, but I do know what Martin Luther had to say about God's presence in this Supper. Luther emphasized that in, with, and under the bread and wine—in the action of eating the bread and drinking the wine—we participate in a witness and a proclamation that Jesus is truly and really present in us for the life of the world.

Indeed, every time we partake of the Lord's Supper we confront a great mystery—the mystery of Jesus' presence. It is a wonderful mystery, a true mystery that has a hold of us by faith. All that Jesus accomplished and all that Jesus promised is celebrated and shared anew every time we come to the Lord's Table. Here God's presence in the bread and wine is affirmed and proclaimed, confessed and celebrated to be God-in-us, God-with-us, and God-under-us.

"This is my body given *for you*. This is my blood shed *for you*," Jesus assures us. But such assurance does not give us license to claim Jesus only for ourselves, nor to hoard the blessings of this meal. It is our privilege and our responsibility, having been nourished with Jesus' body and blood, to depart from the Lord's Table to act on behalf of Jesus, the Living Bread, to feed a world hungry not only for a meal but for meaning, hungry not only for today but for tomorrow.

Bread for a Hungry World

So, how shall we be about this business of feeding a hungry world? We find a model in Jesus' own actions on the night before his crucifixion:

And during supper Jesus, knowing that the Father had given all things into his hands, and that he had come from God and was going to God, got up from the table, took off his outer robe, and tied a towel around himself. Then he poured water into a basin and began to wash the disciples' feet and to wipe them with the towel that was tied around him. (John 13:2-5)

Amazing! The host of the supper took a towel and assumed the role of a servant, washing the feet of his guests. When Peter protested, Jesus rebuked him saying, "Unless I wash you, you have no share with me" (John 13:8). When the disciples did not understand, Jesus explained that he had given them an example. Just as he, their Teacher and Lord, had washed their feet, so they were to wash one another's feet.

Jesus' example is for twenty-first century disciples, too. Our Lord not only invites us to be his guests at his Supper, he sends us out to be *living bread* according to his example, making the world a better place through humble acts of love, compassion, and service.

A story is told about a business executive who was so disillusioned by the incessant demands of his job and the pressures of working in a difficult environment that he had just about given up trying to live according to Jesus' example in his daily life. However, one morning while preparing for yet another busy day, the man promised himself that he would try very hard that day to bear witness to Jesus in his words and actions. A few minutes later, he set out to catch the train into work.

The man thought he had left home in plenty of time, but by the time he had purchased his ticket, he realized that he was running late and would have to hurry to catch the train. Charging across the lobby, he bounded down the last few steps just as the conductor called, "All aboard!" In a mad dash to board the train, the businessman bumped into a small child carrying a jigsaw puzzle. Pieces scattered everywhere.

The man paused, saw the child in tears, and looked again at the train doors that were about to close. With an inward sigh, he walked toward the child, smiled, and bent down to help him pick up the puzzle pieces. As he did, the train pulled out of the station.

The child watched the man intently as they worked together to retrieve all the pieces. After the last piece had been placed safely inside the puzzle box, the little boy looked with awe at the man, and asked, hesitantly, "Mister, are you Jesus?"

Are you Jesus? The question caught the man off-guard. But then he realized that for that moment, in that place, with that child, under those circumstances, through his actions he had, indeed, been Jesus.

Food That Satisfies

When I was growing up, it was common to refer to money as "dough." I remember thinking that I was making big dough on my paper route, and I enjoyed having enough dough to purchase candy for my pals and me after playing baseball all afternoon. I think it's interesting that dough is slang for money because though we can't eat money, we can use it to purchase our daily bread as well as all the other things we need to live from day to day.

Our work not only provides us with the means to take care of our own needs but also gives us the opportunity to share generously with those who are not able to provide life's necessities for themselves. Through the privilege our work affords us to share God's gifts with others, we come to understand that daily work is also God's gift to us. Our work offers us opportunity to serve the needs of others according to Jesus' example.

But if we look around, we quickly realize that the world hungers for far more than food to feed physical bodies. Sales of spirituality and self-help books are rampant. Credit cards are at maximum limits, and we are told repeatedly that our national economic health is dependent upon ever increasing consumer spending. Americans, on average, spend more than four hours each day watching television, surfing the net, or playing video games. It seems apparent that, starved for real food that gives life meaning and purpose, we feed constantly on food that sates our immediate hunger but provides no lasting nourishment.

"Why do you spend your money for that which is not bread," the prophet Isaiah asked, "and your labor for that which does not satisfy?" (Isaiah 55:2). Why, indeed, do we pour time and money into things that can only make us hungrier?

The miracle story of the feeding of the five thousand is recorded in all four New Testament Gospels (Matthew 14:13-21, Mark 6:30-44, Luke 9:10-17, and John 6:1-13). On one level this story is about a time when Jesus—with the help of his disciples—fed a crowd of people who hadn't eaten all day a simple meal of fish and barley bread. Of course, there's much more to the story. The Gospels tell us that Jesus blessed the five loaves and two fish and gave them to the disciples to distribute. The people ate until they were satisfied, and then Jesus commanded the disciples to go among them to gather up all the leftover food "so that nothing [would] be lost" (John 5:12). The disciples did as they were told and the remnants they gathered filled twelve baskets!

In the same way, we receive only a bit of bread and a sip of wine in the Lord's Supper, but it is enough. Enough to satisfy our own need with plenty left over to feed a world starving for far more than daily bread.

> I was hungry and you gave me food, I was thirsty and you gave me something to drink, I was a stranger and you welcomed me, I was naked and you gave me clothing, I was sick and you took care of me, I was in prison and you visited me. (Matthew 25:35-36)

Through Jesus' death on the cross, God enters into the suffering of the world in a very concrete way, and through those who are in need, God continues to confront us today. Here in the heart and needs of the real human family we find God's invitation to share our plenty because God gives us everything.

Recalling Jesus' lesson for us in these verses from the Gospel of Matthew, we are to seek justice, love, and mercy on behalf of all who are hungry, all who are oppressed, rejected, or abused, all who suffer in countless other ways. We see here in Jesus' teaching our sacramental connection to Jesus and to all of our sisters and brothers in God's human family.

The Apostle Paul reminds us that even though Jesus came into this world through God's people Israel, because of Jesus there is neither "Jew nor Greek, slave nor free, male nor female"—for all are one in Christ Jesus (Galatians 3:28). Freed from the power of sin and death through Jesus' death and resurrection, we are bound to Jesus and to one another in a community called the Body of Christ. As the visible sign of God's presence in the world, the Body of Christ gathers to hear God's Word and to share the Sacraments and then disperses into the world to witness to God's redeeming love in Christ Jesus through our words and our deeds.

It is not easy being Jesus' followers in a world filled with problems, pain, fear, and strife. The road we travel is long and hard, and we are tempted to depend on our own strength and courage and belief that we can do the right thing. But we dare not travel alone for the way will be too much for us. Jesus has traveled the road before us. He understands how difficult it is, and so he gives himself to us as bread for the journey.

In the Lord's Supper, Jesus comes to us in a bit of bread and a sip of wine, offering forgiveness and bringing peace and joy. Indeed, this meal primes our lives as wellsprings for faithful living. Nourished by the blessings and promises in his Supper, we take our towels and go out to feed a hungry world with food that satisfies. Empowered by

Christ's body and blood, we work to extend justice, love, and mercy to all who suffer, offering hope for a future that belongs to God, and inviting all people into the fullness of life in the one who is the Bread of Life.

Questions for Discussion

1. What does it mean to you that we are only guests of God in this world? What is the connection of this insight with the Lord's Supper?

2. How can Jesus be present in the Lord's Supper? How can Jesus give us his flesh in this meal?

3. How is Jesus the Bread of Life for the world?

4. How are we, blessed and nourished by the Bread of life, to be the bread of life in the needs of the world?

5. How has the meaning of the petition in the Lord's Prayer, "give us this day our daily bread," changed for you by reading this chapter?

The Lord's Supper is a visible sign of God's gracious will in Jesus to forgive, to heal, to renew our life together, to guide us into abundant living, and to provide us with new life beyond the tomb in God's eternal tomorrow.

5

The Lord's Supper Is a Foretaste of the Feast to Come

On this mountain the Lord of hosts will make for all peoples
a feast of rich food, a feast of well-aged wines,
of rich food filled with marrow, of well-aged wines strained clear.
And he will destroy on this mountain
the shroud that is cast over all peoples,
the sheet that is spread over all nations;
he will swallow up death forever. (Isaiah 25:6-8)

"Truly I tell you, I will never again drink of the fruit of the vine until that day when I drink it new in the kingdom of God." (Mark 14:25)

Central to Jewish faith and hope is the vision of the day when God will act in history to save God's chosen people. We see this in Isaiah's eschatological vision of a banquet that proclaims a future with God that is wholly different from the present in Isaiah's time or our own. Perhaps as Jesus ate the Passover meal together with his disciples they recalled Isaiah's vision and wondered, "Might this be the promised Messiah, the one for whom we have waited?" From our vantage point as an Easter people, we know that Jesus is the Messiah—though not as anticipated. He comes as suffering servant and savior, not at the head of a liberating army but leading a procession carrying his own cross. Jesus is the Savior of all people. Our redemption, salvation, and freedom are won not through a military victory, but through the giving of a life, Jesus' innocent suffering and death.

This final reflection on the Lord's Supper and its meaning for our lives considers the themes of peace and reconciliation, hallmarks of the kingdom of God that was ushered in when Jesus came to live among us but only to be realized fully with his return at the end of time. In this simple meal of bread and wine we are given a foretaste of the heavenly feast to come.

> "Peace I leave with you; my peace I give to you. I do not give to you as the world gives. Do not let your hearts be troubled, and do not let them be afraid." (John 14:27)

The Lord's Supper is a visible sign of God's gracious will in Jesus to forgive, to heal, to renew our life together, to guide us into abundant living, and to provide us with new life beyond the tomb in God's eternal tomorrow. In this meal, Jesus comes to us in our brokenness and need, bringing reconciliation and abundance. In this meal, God gathers us together in a wide embrace and gives us a glimpse of a future where all things are made new.

The Peace of Christ Be with You

In our worship, it is customary to share the peace with one another. In ancient times, this would have involved an embrace or even a kiss. Today we most often settle for a handshake, but the intent is the same. Here we reach out to one another—acquaintance and stranger, friend and foe—in peace.

But what is this peace that we offer?

One of my most treasured possessions is a work of art that I've had for many, many years. The "canvas" is actually a nun's habit, torn into yard-long strips and adorned with a variety of symbols. On each strip, appliqué letters in various sizes and fonts spell out the word, *shalom—peace*. I find very interesting the responses this artwork elicits from those who view it. A few see beyond the crude craftsmanship to the deeper message the artist sought to convey, but most, though polite in their comments, truly cannot appreciate the work because they do not comprehend it. In the same way, we fail to comprehend peace in its fullest expression, peace as Jesus gives it.

Peace means different things to different people. For some, peace is a moment of rest in the midst of the daily hassles of life. For others, it is a feeling of contentment in the coziness of one's own home. Peace can be a sense of transcendence experienced in the beauty of creation. It may be the absence of anger or reprieve from hate. Surely peace is a truce in strained relationships, whether between individuals, peoples, or nations.

"Peace I leave with you," Jesus promises. "My peace I give to you. I do not give to you as the world gives" (John 14:27). What is this peace that Jesus gives that is unlike our own understandings of peace?

The word for peace that Jesus used was *shalom*, a word from ancient times that is still used today as the traditional Jewish form of greeting. It is spoken between passers-by on the street and offered in casual parting, but it means much more than a simple hello or good-bye. We are told that Jewish mothers, upon being separated from their children at Nazi concentration camps, whispered in parting, "Shalom! Shalom!" Family members reunited in Haifa or Tel-Aviv after the war looked at each other, and then broke the silence with "Shalom!" Surely a word that can be used both in times of wrenching grief and overwhelming joy is richer in overtones and depth of meaning than our meager images of peace.

To wish someone shalom is to bestow upon them the blessing, *God be with you.* Even more it is to wish, *God be between you and me,* holding us together, reducing distance. In essence, to wish someone shalom is to acknowledge the truth that it cannot be well with me if it is not well with you. Shalom—peace—when understood in this manner binds our existence and our wellbeing to that of the other.

The peace that Jesus offers is not a state of mind, nor is it the presence of one thing or the absence of something else. The peace that Jesus gives is something wholly new. We have this description from the prophet Isaiah.

> For I am about to create new heavens
> and a new earth;
> the former things shall not be remembered
> or come to mind.
> But be glad and rejoice forever
> in what I am creating;
> for I am about to create Jerusalem as a joy,
> and its people as a delight.
> They shall build houses and inhabit them;
> they shall plant vineyards and eat their fruit.
> They shall not build and another inhabit;
> they shall not plant and another eat;
> for like the days of a tree shall the days of my people be,
> and my chosen shall long enjoy the work of their hands.
> They shall not labor in vain,
> or bear children for calamity;
> for they shall be offspring blessed by the Lord—
> and their descendents as well.
> Before they call I will answer,
> while they are yet speaking I will hear.
> The wolf and the lamb shall feed together,
> the lion shall eat straw like the ox;
> but the serpent—its food shall be dust!
> They shall not hurt or destroy
> on all my holy mountain, says the Lord. (Isaiah 65:17-18, 21-25)

This is shalom! This is peace! It is a new heaven and a new earth where all of creation shares in God's redemption and reclaiming of God's chosen people, a redeemed people reconciled to God and one another, building together the fullness of life in the kingdom of God. This is the peace that the Prince of Peace gives us through his death on a cross and his resurrection on Easter morning. This is the peace that we receive as we share in the Supper instituted by our Lord and Savior, Jesus Christ.

> So if anyone is in Christ, there is a new creation: everything old has passed away; see everything has become new! All this is from God, who reconciled us to himself through Christ, and has given us the ministry of reconciliation; that is, in Christ God was reconciling the world to himself, not counting their trespasses against them, and entrusting the message of reconciliation to us. (2 Corinthians 5:17-19)

Jesus commands us under the new covenant to receive faithfully the Lord's Supper to strengthen our unity with him and with one another as we make real and visible a new community of reconciliation. Because God loves us, we love one another. Because we have been reconciled to God through the death and resurrection of Jesus, we are in turn reconciled to one another. It is this reality that we celebrate in the Lord's Supper.

To be sure, there are differences of opinion concerning the meaning of the Lord's Supper that are nearly as old as the meal itself. These differences of opinion can create strife if we let them. Some traditions put the emphasis in the Supper on repentance, others on Jesus' sacrifice. Still others stress its importance as a time of fellowship and joy. These differences of interpretation and emphasis make for spirited and earnest conversation about the Lord's Supper. But too often we allow these differences to divide the Christian community and to exclude from the meal those whom we deem "unworthy" on the basis of our own interpretation, legalism, or prejudice. Such practice, we have seen, is contrary to Jesus' action in the Upper Room where all disciples, regardless of past failures or future intents, were included in the meal.

Whether a Lutheran Holy Communion, a Methodist Memorial Feast, a Catholic Mass, an Episcopalian Eucharist, or a Community Church Friendship Meal, we come together for this meal because Jesus invites us. This is, after all, the *Lord's* Supper. This Supper of grace was meant to unite all people in God's love for the whole human family. After all, we don't get to choose those with whom we walk or by whom we kneel. We have no say over who hears the words, "given for you," before and after they are said to us. When we participate in this Supper we share and keep alive this good news for all people, until the day when we celebrate together with Christ the banquet feast of eternal life.

Jesus is the bringer of peace. He both encourages and initiates shalom. We who partake of his Supper are to be a living expression of the peace of God accomplished in Jesus the Christ. Any sharing of Jesus' Supper in Jesus' name should not be less than an expression and an experience of this new community of God's peace in the world today.

Living Together in Community

Jesus has brought us together into a new kind of community with all the rich overtones of shalom, of peace. The Supper celebrates this reality, creates it, and empowers it to fuller expression. But it is not enough that we who gather at the Lord's Table be reconciled to one another. We are called to a ministry of reconciliation, and we are entrusted with bringing peace to a world abounding with hate, strife, want, and war. Affirmed, nourished, and empowered by the food of the Supper, we are called to serve as ambassadors for the Prince of Peace.

To be an authentic witness of God's reconciling power in the world, we must first strive to be reconciled with one another in the church. Here are Jesus' words on this matter.

"So when you are offering your gift at the altar, if you remember that your brother or sister has something against you, leave your gift there before the altar and go; first be reconciled to your brother or sister, and then come and offer your gift." (Matthew 5:23-24)

We who have been given Christ's continuing ministry of peace and reconciliation have not always carried out the task faithfully or well. Though we set out with good intentions, our mission has been clouded by cultural pressures and false teachings, as well as by organizational and political issues within the community of believers. We are all products of our culture and our faith traditions. Often, our theologies, our prejudices, and our fears can and do block and limit the expression and experience of the Lord's Supper. Thus there is a continuing need to review and reformulate our practices and life together in his community according to Jesus' example and intentions, including our use and sharing of the Lord's Supper.

We may think that love is optional and reconciling with our neighbor is something we can choose to do or not to do. Neither is the case. "Love one another," Jesus commands. "As you have been forgiven, forgive."

A Foretaste of the Feast to Come

Indeed, we have been invited into Jesus' passion story of self-giving love by the splashing of water and kept there with wine and bread shared in the name of Jesus—with a cross and an empty tomb in the center of it all.

According to legend, it was once a tradition for families of wealthy Christians to leave food on the graves of loved ones after their burial. The food wasn't intended as provisions for the dead, like in some cultures, but rather as a feast for the living. After family members departed, poor and hungry people would gather at the graves to eat and drink and offer prayers of thanksgiving for the life of the one who had died. In the eating and drinking among the tombstones, life continued.

There will be tombs—both figurative and literal—in our lives, but because of Jesus, death will not have the final word. We have been promised a future with God where there will be no mourning or crying or pain or death, a future where we will be reconciled to one another and the whole of creation, a future where all things will be made new.

Throughout the course of my ministry, I've presided over the Lord's Supper in worship settings, at hospital bedsides, and in the homes of homebound believers. It has been my privilege on numerous occasions to share Jesus' special meal with people who were nearing the end of their earthly life. I remember especially Kristin, a beautiful twelve-year-old girl in my Woodinville, Washington, parish.

Kirsten had the most beautiful eyes imaginable. They reflected her spirit of peace, courage, and hope in spite of the fact that she suffered with Ewing's Sarcoma, a very rare and deadly form of cancer. Following sixteen months of chemotherapy, radiation treatments, and enrollment in a clinical trial, Kirsten passed on to the promised Easter life announced for her in her baptism and remembered often in our conversations while sharing the Lord's Supper during the closing months of her young life.

Before her death, Kirsten wrote and gave me the following poem. It is her testimony to the gospel's gifts and promises, to the blessings and benefits of the Lord's Supper being a foretaste of the feast to come.

A World of Hope
I hold in my hand
a world of hope,
a world of peace,
a world to cope.

In this world are many treasures,
happiness, joy and lots of pleasures.
You'll never hear a discouraging word,
Only compliments will be heard.
Disease is foreign in this place,
Unhappy frowns aren't seen on any face.
Summer and flowers are always in bloom,
There's never a single cloud of gloom.
Follow the rainbow and you will find,
this life full of wonders of every kind.
I hold in my hand
a world of hope,
a world of peace,
a world to cope.
—Kirsten Gould

In the Lord's Supper we are given a glimpse of the future that Kirsten now knows. In a bit of bread and a sip of wine we are given a foretaste of the glorious feast to come and assured that as there is life beyond the tomb for Jesus, so there will be for us. Dine often, for in this meal are blessings for today, nourishment along our way, and promises for tomorrow…given for you.

Questions for Discussion

1. What images come to mind when you hear the word *peace*?

2. How has reading this chapter changed your view of what peace means?

3. What factors make for peace? What is our calling to be peace-makers?

4. Discuss a situation where reconciliation brought peace to you or someone you know.

5. How is the Lord's Supper *a tomb-transcending meal* for us?

6. How do you understand the Lord's Supper to be an Easter Meal? A foretaste of the feast to come?

Appendix

Eleven Reflections on the Lord's Supper

The holistic vision of the meaning of the Lord's Supper presented in this book was shaped by eleven facets of meaning given in lectures many years ago by the late Dr. Kent Knutson, Professor of Church Doctrine at Luther Seminary in St. Paul, Minnesota. Dr. Knutson later served as President of Wartburg Theological Seminary, in Dubuque, Iowa, and as the first president of the former American Lutheran Church (ALC), a predecessor church body to the present ELCA. The following eleven perspectives were gleaned from reading again my class notes from this favorite mentor. Dr. Knutson nurtured in me my theological foundations and perspectives. Honed and matured over my years of ministry, study, and research, these perspectives are still affirmed and reflected in this book.

> [T]he Lord Jesus on the night when he was betrayed took a loaf of bread, and when he had given thanks, he broke it and said, "This is my body that is for you. *Do this in remembrance of me.*" In the same way he took the cup also, after supper, saying, "This cup is the new covenant in my blood. *Do this, as often as you drink it, in remembrance of me.*" For as often as you eat this bread and drink the cup, you proclaim the Lord's death until he comes. (1 Corinthians 11:23-26, italics added)

1. *The Lord's Supper is gospel, not law.* It is God's gracious gift given to us to sustain our new life as the forgiven ones in Christ. The Supper does not demand perfection on our part to be worthy of its reception. Its purpose is not to judge, but to comfort; not to divide the people of God in the human family, but to unite; not to fill our hearts with terror, but with joy.

2. *The Lord's Supper is a sign.* It is a visible sign of God's gracious will to forgive all people. It is a visible sign to the person of faith that God is personally present. It is a sign of remembrance of the blood of the cross shed for us, of Jesus as the true Bread of Life given for us, of the suffering on the cross for us, and of the banquet feast yet to come.

3. *The Lord's Supper is a sacrament of renewal.* While baptism is the sacrament by which we are initiated into new life in God, the Lord's Supper strengthens, deepens, and renews that life each time we partake of the meal.

4. *The Lord's Supper is participation in the community of Jesus' followers.* It involves not only communion with the personal presence of Jesus, our Lord and Savior, but also a witness of the fellowship that should exist among the individuals who are followers of the Lord of life.

5. *The Lord's Supper is a memorial feast.* The same person who lived, died, and rose again for our new life now and for our eternal life is the one who comes to us through the bread and wine. The Lord's Supper identifies the community of Christ in the world today, a community of faith in Jesus as Lord and Savior that arose out of the event of the cross and the resurrection. As we participate in this supper, we identify with all of Christ's own people who have gathered in the fellowship of this sacrament down through the centuries.

6. *The Lord's Supper is an act of confession.* Knowing our need for renewal through forgiveness, we go to meet the risen Christ. Just as we also encounter Jesus in the Word and in our lives and the lives of others each day, now we meet Christ in this visible and more dramatic way. It is still Christ's action, Christ's supper, but we go in

boldness to the table of grace. The initiative is now ours as much as it is Jesus'. We do something too: *We must go.* Why? Because Jesus invites and Jesus waits for our coming. And, in so going, we witness to Jesus' life, death, and resurrection for us. This act of our going is not a meritorious work, but we must decide. We must go as a response to the invitation.

7. *The Lord's Supper is a sacrament of repentance.* The sacrament is for the penitent, but it does not demand some fresh sin to confess before one needs to come. It is a repentance that acknowledges that, while we live in grace, we also live in sin. The penitent are all who believe in a dependence on God's forgiveness in life. We must not go in remorse to the Lord's Supper, though we always go as sinners. Yet we are sinners who already are justified as the forgiven ones in Jesus Christ and who trust joyfully in what one receives in the sacrament. The Lord's Supper is not a sacrament to fit only emotional needs once in awhile; it should be a regular part of the Christian life. *Do this in remembrance of me!*

8. *The Lord's Supper is a sacrament of joy.* We so often forget this aspect—the celebration of joy. The sacrament is a celebration not only of the cross but also of the resurrection. It is the Risen One, the living God, who comes to us in the receiving of the bread and wine in this simple meal.

9. *The Lord's Supper is a sacrament of the continued Christian life.* God is always present in the church, that is, in God's people, and not only in the sacrament. The effects of the sacrament are not confined to the moment but go on into the future. Thus, we do not believe that we must have the sacrament every day to live in God's grace. On the other hand, we ought to frequently accept Jesus' invitation: *Do this, as often as you do it, in remembrance of me!*

10. *The Lord's Supper is the mode of Jesus' body and blood.* There is a point of mystery here of grace and faith. The personal presence of Jesus in the experience of the sacrament must be accepted in the simplicity of faith. It is an act of confessing Jesus' presence for the forgiveness of sin. It is not an act on our part that should demand a scientific explanation of *the how.* We come in faith with the expectation of meeting Jesus and knowing that we are the forgiven ones.

11. *The Lord's Supper is a sacrament of hope.* As we come, we remember the past event of Jesus' life, death, and resurrection for us in the present experience of the sacrament. We look forward in hope to that which is promised to come. That which is not yet completed in God's new creation is celebrated now, enjoyed now, and experienced now, as a foretaste of the fellowship and communion with God and one another that will continue in our resurrection life—in the likeness of the sign seen in the risen Jesus!

Glossary

My hope is that this book may be a teaching and preaching resource as well as a helpful guide for those interested in studying and discussing the meaning and use of the Lord's Supper. It is helpful to come into a discussion speaking the same language. To that end, I offer the following glossary so that all participants may have the same understanding of basic terms associated with the sacrament.

acquittal: the act by which we are set free from our sin through God's yes of forgiveness. Our acquittal comes from the cross, upon which our broken relationship with God is restored as a reality now and as the basis of our inheritance of eternal life.

breaking of bread: the description used by Luke repeatedly in the book of Acts for the Lord's Supper.

Bread of Life: a name for Jesus that refers to the spiritual food we need in order to live for time and eternity. In John, chapter 6, Jesus refers to himself as both *the bread of life* and *the bread from heaven*, a reference back to the manna God gave the Israelites in the wilderness. Unlike the manna the Israelites needed each day, Jesus, as Bread of Life, offers a once and for all new covenant with God's people that nourishes forgiveness and new life through God's love and grace.

bread for tomorrow: a description for all things that through Jesus will be our inheritance in God's creation made new and whole forever. (Related terms: *the banquet feast, life to come, the kingdom of heaven, the Easter life, eternal life*.)

confession: admitting one's sins to God and seeking absolution. In Lutheran liturgy, the Confession and Absolution customarily happen before the Lord's Supper is celebrated.

Easter life: eternal life made possible by Christ's death and resurrection.

elements of the Lord's Supper/Communion elements: refers to the bread (the body of Christ) and wine (the blood of Christ) used in Holy Communion. Some churches use grape juice instead of wine.

feast to come: refers to life with God in eternity or life in heaven.

forgiveness: God's claiming and accepting love expressed toward the whole human family through Jesus' life, death, and resurrection, which establishes our new and lasting relationship with God and is the sole basis of our promised gift of life eternal.

The Apostle Paul emphasizes in his writings that *the forgiveness of sins* constitutes the redemption of the human race effected by the death of Jesus (see Ephesians 1:7-8; Colossians 1:13-14).

gospel: literally from the Greek, gospel means "good news." The New Testament understanding of gospel is the good news that all people are saved from their sins through God's unconditional love, goodwill, and mercy as shown through Christ's death on the cross. The gospel frees us from the ultimate consequences of our sins and changes our destiny from death to promised new life with Christ forever. See also, *law*.

gospel covenant: God's new relationship with the human family through the death of Jesus on the cross. The new covenant established and maintained by God's gracious, unconditional love taught and acted out through God's personal presence in Jesus.

grace: God's unconditional, redemptive love for the human family, apart from any merit, through the life, death, and resurrection of Jesus.

kingdom of heaven/kingdom of God: refers to the reign of God, ushered in by Christ, which is both present and future. The kingdom is a spiritual one found where God rules in the hearts of people. It will culminate in eternity, when we are together with God.

Lamb of God: Jesus is the provided sacrificial lamb by God on the cross for the salvation of the world. Also called: *the Passover lamb, the paschal lamb.*

law: the words of God that tell God's people what to do in their relationships with God, with one another, and toward all people. The law shows us our wrongdoings and need of change, correction, and God's forgiveness. This understanding is used most often in contrast to the gospel, God's grace and forgiveness.

Lord's Supper: one of two sacraments in the Reformation heritage of the Christian church—the sacraments of Baptism and the Lord's Supper, or Holy Communion. The Lord's Supper is the most common name for the simple meal instituted by Jesus in the Upper Room in Jerusalem while participating in the Passover meal with his disciples before his arrest, trial, and crucifixion (see Matthew 26:17-29; Mark 14:22-25; Luke 22:14-20; 1 Corinthians 11:23-26). In this meal, Jesus is both the host and the food of blessing, nourishment, and promise. Bread and wine, the two elements in this simple meal, are the means of God's grace through Jesus Christ. Other names for this meal: *Holy Communion, Eucharist, Sacred Mass, Memorial Feast, the Lamb's Supper, the Jesus Meal, Fellowship Meal, Fiesta Meal.*

Lord's Table/the Table: another name for the Lord's Supper or Holy Communion.

manna: the daily food provided by God during the Hebrew tribes wandering in the desert from Egypt to the Promised Land, during the Exodus. Jesus is *the manna from heaven* in the new covenant story. Manna or bread from heaven is a dominant symbol related to Jesus in John's Gospel (see John 6:51).

means of grace: the means by which God calls people to faith. The Lutheran tradition identifies the Word of God and the Sacraments of Baptism and Holy Communion as means of grace.

new covenant: God's new relationship with the human family, which Jesus announced was the purpose for this life's work, death, and resurrection (see Matthew 26:26-29). This relationship is not based on the law, but on God's grace as shown through Jesus' saving act.

Passover meal: the central festival meal for the Jewish faith community, first shared on the night before Moses led the Israelites out of Egypt. God instructed the Israelites to mark their door frames with blood from a sacrificed lamb, and observing this marking, the angel of death would pass over their homes. God commanded that this redemptive act be remembered through an annual Passover meal celebrated on the anniversary of their deliverance (see Exodus 12, Deuteronomy 16:1-8). Also called: *Seder meal, the Feast of Unleavened Bread* (the Passover and the annual Feast of Unleavened Bread were blended into one meal of remembrance and gratitude following the Exodus).

repentance: a change of mind that results in a change of direction. More than feeling sorry for one's sins, the biblical understanding of repentance is a continual turning from a life of disobedience to an obedient way of thinking and living that results in a renewed relationship with God and with one another.

reconciliation: restoration to a covenant relationship with God.

Seder: see Passover meal.

shalom: a Hebrew word generally translated as "peace." In larger context it refers to God's action of peacemaking and harmonizing in and for the world through Jesus. Jesus' model of peace, joy, and servant love serve as a sign and promise to the human family of a new community already present in the world through those who see and respond to the gospel and in the future shalom community where God shall make all things new, whole, and harmonized forever. The Lord's Supper is the communal meal of this new shalom community in today's world.

Upper Room: the site of Jesus' last supper with his disciples, where the Lord's Supper was established for all people. The event took place in an upper room in a house in Jerusalem.

Word: can refer to the written Word of God (the Bible) or the Word made flesh (Jesus).

Additional Resources

Come to God's Table: Preparing for Holy Communion. Minneapolis: Augsburg Fortress, 1989.

This five-session educational series containing three booklets (student, parent, and leader guide) is designed to help fifth and sixth graders and their parents discover the connection between Baptism and Holy Communion.

Eating and Drinking in the Word: The Sacrament of Holy Communion. Minneapolis: Augsburg Fortress Video #15-9691.

This fifteen-minute long video presents a Lutheran understanding of Communion to grades 4-6 and above. Great for use with confirmation and new member classes.

Grace Community Church and SpiritFilms. *Igniting Worship Series: Communion.* Nashville: Abingdon Press, 2003.

DVD resource to assist pastors and worship leaders in building an effective worship experience. This DVD contains ten Communion worship experiences organized around a Scripture passage and theme, and includes brief biblical and liturgical comments, sermon outlines, calls to worship, prayers, and benedictions.

Holy Communion. Chicago: elca.org/Mosaic Television, 2006.

Featuring the insights of Lutheran School of Theology at Chicago scholars Craig A. Satterlee and Kurt K. Hendel, this DVD explores the biblical foundations for Holy Communion, and reviews the Reformation history that defines modern Christian understandings of Holy Communion. Available online at www.elca.org/mosaic/HolyCommunion/index.html.

Marty, Martin E. *The Lord's Supper: Expanded Edition.* Minneapolis: Augsburg Fortress Press, 1997.

Marty describes the origins of Holy Communion and the important role this sacrament has played throughout the history of the Christian church. This classic book on Holy Communion features a new study guide to help individual readers and study groups ponder the meaning of this Christian sacrament.

Patton, John. *Is Human Forgiveness Possible?* Academic Renewal Press, 2003.

This book addresses the difficulty Christians can have in forgiving others. Patton uses case studies from his pastoral counseling practice to discuss the problem and to offers solutions.

Places in the Heart. Sony Pictures, 2001.

Set in the South during the Great Depression, this film tells the gripping story of a young widow and her family who try to run their cotton farm with the help of a disparate group of friends. The closing scene of this powerful movie illustrates the reconciling, transforming power of Christ's presence with us in this special meal.

Porter, Thomas W., ed. *Conflict and Communion: Reconciliation and Restorative Justice at Christ's Table.* Nashville: Upper Room Books, 2006.

A collection of essays on justice and Holy Communion written by a group of ecumenical contributors. Nashville, Discipleship Resources, 2006.

Skinner, Douglas B. *At the Lord's Table: Communion Prayers for All Seasons.* St. Louis: Chalice Press, 2006.

Skinner anchors this collection of nearly 200 prayers with biblical references. Prayers for the bread and for the cup are linked with special Sundays, church seasons, hymns, special occasions, and communion themes.

Smedes, Lewis B. *Forgive & Forget: Healing the Hurts We Don't Deserve.* San Francisco: Harper Collins Paperback Edition, 1996. In this book the author breaks down the healing process into four steps and uses real-life stories to offer solace and hope to those who long for the peace that comes with forgiveness.

Torvend, Samuel. *Daily Bread, Holy Meal: Opening the Gifts of Holy Communion.* Minneapolis: Augsburg Fortress, 2004. This exploration of the Eucharist asks the seeker in every Christian to consider the ecological, theological, communal, and ethical dimensions of the Lord's Supper.

The Use of theMeans of Grace: A Statement on the Practice of Word and Sacrament. Minneapolis: Augsburg Fortress, 1997. This statement was adopted for guidance and practice by the Fifth Biennial Churchwide Assembly of the Evangelical Lutheran Church in America, August 19, 1997. This document provides guidance on the proclamation of the Word and the Christian assembly, on Holy Baptism, on Holy Communion, and on the relationship between worship and Christian mission. Available online at www.elca.org/worship/worship/sacraments/umg.html.

Wallace, Robin Knowles. *Communion Services (Just In Time!).* Nashville: Abingdon Press, 2006. This book introduces the practice of Communion and offers a collection of Communion prayers and ready-to-use resources for worship. Knowles is an associate professor of worship and music at Methodist Theological Seminary in Ohio.

Willimon, William H. *Sunday Dinner: The Lord's Supper and the Christian Life.* Nashville: Upper Room Books, 1981.

A book for those who want to explore the meaning of the gift of the Lord's Supper and its significance for their daily lives as Christians. Written for laypersons, clergy, and seminary students, this book also includes a group study guide for each chapter.

Wright, Tom. *The Meal Jesus Gave Us: Understanding Holy Communion.* Louisville: Westminster John Knox Press, 2003.

Written by Anglican scholar and Bishop of Durham, this is an introduction to the Lord's Supper suitable for new member and confirmation classes. The book is divided into two sections covering the early historical development of the Eucharistic and the theology of the Eucharist.

www.elca.org/worship/worship/sacraments/communion.html

This ELCA web page lists helpful links to articles and other resources related to Holy Communion. Included is a list of frequently asked questions concerning Holy Communion practices in the Lutheran church.